Disney · PIXAR
FINDING NEMO

The Essential Guide

Written by Simon Beecroft and Glenn Dakin
Designed by Guy Harvey
Assistant Art Editors Ishita Chawla, Akansha Jain
Additional Editorial Assistance Tina Jindal, Victoria Taylor
Senior Pre-production Producer Jennifer Murray
DTP Designer Umesh Singh Rawat, Eric Shapland
Managing Editors Sadie Smith, Chitra Subramanyam
Design Managers Neha Ahuja, Ron Stobbart
Art Director Lisa Lanzarini
Publisher Julie Ferris
Publishing Director Simon Beecroft

First published in Great Britain in 2003
This edition published in Great Britain in 2016 by
Dorling Kindersley Limited
80 Strand, London WC2R 0RL
A Penguin Random House Company

Contains content previously published in *Finding Nemo: The Essential Guide* (2003) and *Finding Nemo: The Ultimate Sticker Book* (2003)

10 9 8 7 6 5 4 3 2 1
001–290561–Mar/16

Page design Copyright © 2016 Dorling Kindersley Limited

Copyright © 2016 Disney Enterprises, Inc. and Pixar Animation Studios.

All rights reserved. No part of this publication may be reproduced, stored in a retrieval system or transmitted in any form or by any means, electronic, mechanical, photocopying, recording or otherwise, without the prior written permission of the copyright owner.

A CIP catalogue record for this book
is available from the British Library.

ISBN: 978-0-24124-632-0

Printed and bound in China

www.dk.com
www.pixar.com
www.disney.com

A WORLD OF IDEAS:
SEE ALL THERE IS TO KNOW

DK

Disney · PIXAR

FINDING NEMO

THE ESSENTIAL GUIDE

Written by Simon Beecroft and Glenn Dakin

Contents

Nemo	6	Sunken Sub	34
Marlin	8	The Abyss	36
Dory	10	Moonfish	38
Coral Reef	12	Jellyfish	40
Fish School	14	Turtles	42
School Friends	16	The Whale	44
The Drop-off	18	Sydney Harbour	46
The Tank Gang	20	Deep Sea Stickers	48
More Gang!	22	On The Reef	50
Tank Life	24	Tank Life	52
Dentist's Lobby	26	Shark Shocks!	53
Exam Room	28	Sea Journey	54
Bruce	30	Famous Fish	56
Anchor and Chum	32	Stickers	58

Dive in!

Welcome to Nemo's world, the big beautiful ocean. It's an amazing place, full of some of the most brightly coloured sea creatures you'll ever meet. Join Marlin on his journey from the Great Barrier Reef to Sydney, where he meets the truly amazing animals that live in the warm tropical waters of the Pacific Ocean. It is a sea teeming with forgetful fish, friendly fish, happy fish, angry fish and extremely large fish! Dive into the adventure and if you ever get stuck… just keep swimming!

Nemo

Nemo is a little clownfish with big dreams. Despite being born with a withered fin, Nemo is destined to explore. As a toddler, he would beg for his dad to part the tentacles of their sea anemone home and glimpse the surrounding reef. Now, Nemo can't wait to start school – and he hopes one day to meet a shark!

Nemo's dorsal fin (the one on his back) keeps him floating upright and steady.

Lucky fin

Home Life

Nemo's father, Marlin, keeps a watchful eye on his son. Growing up, they would stay safe inside their anemone home. Now that Nemo is six, it is time for him to start school. His dad says the ocean is not safe, but Nemo thinks he is ready to face the dangers.

Clownfish
Home: Indian & Pacific Oceans
Adult size: 7.5 cm (3 in)
Food: Not fussy eaters
Fact: Clownfish come in a wide range of bright colours.

Nemo's right fin is much smaller than his left fin, so he swims a bit off-balance, but it doesn't slow him down. Marlin calls Nemo's right fin his lucky one. You see, Nemo's mother and siblings were taken away by a hungry barracuda when Nemo was an egg. Nemo survived, but was born with a damaged fin.

Clownfish Home

Fan coral

- A sea anemone makes a nice, safe home for you if you are a clownfish, but don't invite your pals around – your house might sting them!
- Clownfish are protected from the anemone's stings because they brush up against the tentacles every day to get used to them. Nemo has to brush every morning and night just like you!
- Clownfish are the only underwater animals who enjoy this special relationship with anemones.

Nemo's body shape is broken up by white stripes, making him harder for hungry predators to spot.

Nemo uses his tail to push himself along – like having a personal propeller.

Newcomer

Nemo's first day of school is more of an adventure than he ever could have imagined. He finds himself in a dentist's office fish tank complete with Hawaiian tiki heads and a bubbling volcano!

Fish Tank

Nemo meets a unique group of new friends in the dentist's fish tank. The tank's leader, Gill, takes Nemo under his fin and nicknames him "Shark Bait". Gill is from the ocean, like Nemo, and is determined to help Nemo get back to his dad. In fact, with Nemo's help, they might all escape!

Marlin

Nemo's dad Marlin is the most devoted parent on the reef. He's determined to look after Nemo and make sure that nothing bad happens to him. When a human diver catches Nemo, Marlin sets out on a heroic trek to find him, and becomes famous as the ocean's most daring dad. Marlin is proud of being a clownfish, and would be a funny one, too – if anyone ever let him finish a joke!

Devastated by a barracuda attack on his wife and family, Marlin constantly reminds his only son, Nemo, that "Danger is everywhere..."

Marlin asks Nemo how many stripes he has whenever he thinks Nemo might be hurt. However, Nemo knows by now his dad always has three stripes!

Life Story

Marlin was born into a large family in Australia's Great Barrier Reef. One of 103 brothers and sisters, he was constantly trying to get attention by telling jokes – but no one seemed to be laughing. When he finally met a girl fish who found him funny, he decided to stop clowning around and married her pronto.

Marlin makes sure Nemo follows proper procedure when leaving their home. That is: go out of the anemone, look for danger, swim back in, go out, look for danger and back in again... Often, Marlin forgets why they wanted to go out in the first place!

Trust Dory

Marlin meets a blue tang named Dory on his quest to find Nemo. They become friends. In fact, it is Dory who helps Marlin become a better father. She makes him realize that if he never lets anything happen to Nemo… nothing will *ever* happen to him!

A special layer of goo protects clownfish from anemone stings.

Marlin's large eyes are ever-watchful for danger.

Marlin's Top Fears

- **Attack by barracuda:** These spear-toothed eating machines shred first and ask questions later.

- **No one will help him:** All Marlin wants to do is find his son, but friendly fish can be hard to come by. He is especially frustrated by moonfish, who would rather do impressions than give directions.

- **Becoming fish and chips:** Marlin thinks that everything in the sea is waiting to eat him. However, after battling the ocean to rescue his son, he gets nicknamed Superfish... not bad for a fish from the reef.

Marlin is often amazed by his new friend Dory. They found a diver's mask that could be a clue to tracking down his son, they escaped a hungry shark, they survived an explosion... and she still has time to dream of bad haircuts!

Dory

Regal Tang
Home: Indian & Pacific Oceans
Size: 25 cm (10 in)
Temperament: Energetic
Fish fact: Regal tangs enjoy playing with shells!

She may seem to be the ocean's biggest bubblehead, but Dory is one feisty fish with hidden talents! Not much is known about her past, because she can't remember any of it! If you ask Dory about her family she'll probably say, "Sure, I have a big family… hey! Where'd they go?" But Dory always remembers to care about important things, like her friends and helping people in trouble.

Regal tangs start out life yellow, just like Dory's tail is now; they gradually turn blue as they grow up.

Meeting Marlin

Dory and Marlin do not exactly start off as best friends. She promises she can lead him in the right direction to find Nemo. But when Marlin follows her, she forgets what she is doing and tells him to leave her alone!

Reading Human

Marlin and Dory find a clue: a mask with human writing. Luckily, Dory can read it. "P. Sherman, 42 Wallaby Way, Sydney", it says. And for the first time she doesn't forget! She's so excited she repeats the address over and over and over and over…

Dory has bigger eyes than Marlin, as tangs get around more than clownfish and need to see in deeper, murkier places.

New Friends

Dory loves to play games. When a school of moonfish offers to play a game of charades, she can't resist. She is not very talented at charades, often mistaking a clam for an octopus. But it's a good thing she makes friends easily. These moonfish know the way to Sydney, Australia!

One of Dory's very special talents is the ability to speak whale. So far, she's mastered humpback, grey whale and speaks three dialects of orca.

Dory points the tip of her fin toward her mouth when deep in thought.

Dory Data

- **Favourite song:** Keep Swimming (written and composed by Dory!)

- **Hobbies:** Languages – along with whale, Dory can speak 42 fish dialects and is currently studying conversational plankton.

- **Favourite food:** Can't remember.

Tangs use their fins to zoom around real fast.

Coral Reef

The reef is a teeming metropolis, a great city of coral under the sea. It's the place where all the most weird and wonderful fish in the world get together to hang out… and, well, just be fish! It's also home to Nemo and his dad.

Reef Life

Life may look chaotic on the reef near Nemo's home, but really it's a well-organized society. There are swimming lanes instead of traffic lanes, coral stacks instead of apartment blocks and nice sandy beds to sleep in at night.

The Great Barrier Reef is the world's largest coral reef. It is home to 1,500 species of fish and 400 different types of coral. The reef is young compared to other coral reefs – it is only 500,000 years old!

Nemo and Marlin live in a cosy anemone far from the open ocean.

Organ pipe corals extend their feeders at night to grab passing snacks, and close during the day.

Hard corals provide homes for many busy little fish, who defend their own corners against strangers.

Reef Info

• Bright colours on a fish help it to attract a mate. Of course, there's no telling if they'll get along.

• Corals are the snack bars of the sea. Tiny sea plants grow with them and produce a constant source of food. Open 24-7, customers are never turned away, which proves there actually is such a thing as a free lunch!

• Anemones may look rooted to the spot, but if they run short of food, they can slurp off to a new picnic-spot by creeping along on their sucker-like bases – and then eat anything they find there!

• Spanish dancers are reef creatures that flamenco-dance their way out of trouble, flapping the hems of their brightly patterned "skirts" at unwanted followers.

Bright colours are helpful when crossing a busy fish stream at night.

Bert

Attention-grabbing shiny scales

Hutch

Tentacles used to smell food!

Maria the Spanish dancer

Brain corals look like human brains, but they're no smarter than any other corals.

13

Fish School

Fish love to get together in a school! Learning is fun with Mr. Ray in charge, who studied at the world-famous Barrier Reef Fish School. He loves to teach and also to sing. In fact, he sings while he teaches. "My songs have information, my songs have entertainment! Put them together and you get entertain-o-mation!" Judging by the class test score, Mr. Ray's teaching philosophy is paying off!

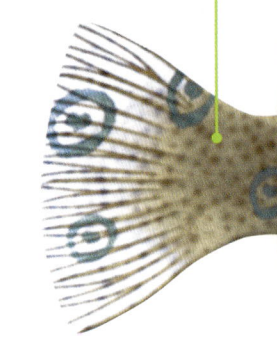

Sand colour good for... well, mainly hiding in the sand

Pay Attention, Class!

Nemo's class is made up of all kinds of reef fish. The children all seem to get along, but Mr. Ray has two strict rules that every student must follow… learn and have fun!

Rays
Home: Seabeds worldwide
Size: up to 8.8 m (28.8 ft) long
Animal group: Rays are related to sharks.
Fact: Rays are known to be intelligent creatures.

Wing-like fins for gliding slowly through the water

Eyes raised above head to see when napping on sandy bottoms

Welcome aboard!
Mr. Ray can't imagine kids finding school boring. He thinks of them not as pupils, but as fellow explorers of the sea. As he likes to sing, "A life of science is filled with wonder, when facts of the sea are ours to plunder!"

Mr. Johannsen

Mr. Johannsen is the neighbourhood grump. This cranky flounder hates it when the reef kids play in his sandy yard. Fortunately, he is never able to catch the kids because he only has eyes on one side of his head!

Large, grumpy mouth

The other dads are surprised to see Marlin finally bringing Nemo to class. Sheldon's dad urges the kids to treat Nemo kindly. "Be nice! It's his first time at school!"

Jumping on Mr. Ray

Mr. Ray is so keen to show his pupils the world about them that he even doubles as a school bus. His wings provide the seating room – just don't stick kelp gum under the seats! Mr Ray also takes the swimming team to their tournaments. Go, Fighting Plankton!

School Life

- The students at reef school don't have books. Instead of a whiteboard, they draw pictures in the sand. At playtime, they use the sponge beds as a trampoline.

- Señor Seaweed is the school's music teacher. The school has lots of instruments, including sand-dollar tambourines, a kelp guitar and a clam drum set. Unfortunately, clams don't appreciate being played!

- Kathy is the class techno-wiz. She dreams of one day inventing a synthetic oxygen lung so she can breathe above water and discover the uncharted territory above the sea.

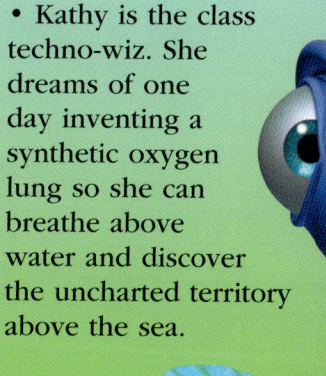

White dots help rays to hide in sand on the sea floor

Strong teeth

School Friends

At first, Nemo's fellow pupils don't seem a very friendly bunch. Tad even tells Nemo he looks funny! But when Marlin explains to the other kids about his son's "lucky" fin, Nemo soon finds out that Pearl has one tentacle slightly shorter than the rest, and that poor Sheldon is "H2O intolerant" (water makes him sneeze!). So Nemo feels right at home with his new pals.

False "eyespot" fools predators into thinking the fish is looking the other way

Some butterfly fish use their fins to leap right out of the water to catch flies!

Butterfly Fish
Home: Coral reefs
Size: 12.5 cm (5 in) long
Food: Use long snout to poke in between rocks for food
Fact: Get their name from their habit of flitting around the reef.

Tad

Tad is a long-nosed butterfly fish who loves to have fun. Because he is so smart, Tad gets bored easily and makes trouble just to get attention. Unfortunately, he often gets caught and has to clean the eraser sponges after class.

Making Friends

"C'mon Nemo!" Nemo soon finds out that his new friends are the coolest kids in the school. And maybe at last he'll discover whether everything his neighbourhood friend, Sandy Plankton, says is true. Sandy told Nemo that turtles live to be a hundred!

On the very edge of the reef, Nemo and his new friends excitedly discuss the sight of a mysterious floating object from the world of humans. Sandy Plankton says it's called a butt. It's actually a boat. Wouldn't it be cool to try and touch it? Big mistake, kids!

Sheldon

A kid seahorse, Sheldon likes to gallop around the reef with his pals. His sneezing sends him backwards all the time, which means he is always the last one to touch base in a game of tag.

Male seahorses give birth to babies!

Curly tail used to grip onto seaweed

Seahorse
Home: Warm waters
Size: 5–36 cm (2–14 in)
Fact: Seahorses swim upright, rapidly waving their fins to move themselves.

Octopuses propel themselves along by sucking water into their bodies and blowing it out again.

Pearl

Pearl is a little flapjack octopus. Her friends like to scare her because octopuses spurt black ink when frightened. (Pearl hates inking in public.) Nonetheless, she is one of the most popular kids at school and is the star football player. She has eight great feet!

Octopus
Home: Atlantic & Pacific Oceans
Size: Up to 45.5 cm (18 in)

The Other Dads

• Tad's dad, Phil, is a long-nosed butterfly fish who had a hard time himself when his first kid started school. Ten kids later, he is an old pro.

• Pearl's father, Ted, is a flapjack octopus. He thinks it is a pity that Marlin is a clownfish who isn't funny.

• Sheldon's dad, Bob, is a seahorse who always keeps a healthy supply of slimy kelp tissues on hand for his H2O-intolerant son. By the way, he doesn't appreciate being called "Pony Boy".

The Drop-off

Welcome to the edge. This is where the reef ends and the unknown realms of the ocean begin. Marlin thought it would be a great place to raise his kids, until they were taken away by a barracuda. When he finds out that his son is headed there on his first school trip, Marlin immediately chases after him.

Nemo!

The Drop-off is the perfect place for divers to anchor their "butts" and explore the reef. Nemo dares to "touch the butt" to spite his father and impress his new friends. But everything goes wrong when a diver captures him by surprise.

Organ pipe corals: warning to tiny life forms – don't stick your ear down there to listen for a tune. There's a live polyp inside that's dying to nab you with its tentacles.

Plate corals provide handy shade on a sunny day, but watch out – dark corners are a great place to meet up with some nasty predators…

Fish Out Of Water!

The diver's boat speeds away, knocking Marlin back in its wake. Marlin gives chase, but already it is too late. The boat is gone. How will he ever find his missing son?

Sea-fan coral branches out into fan-like spreads that can make a great shelter – a good place for tired fish to take a rest from pesky strong currents.

Barrier reefs grow along coasts where the water is warm and shallow. Beyond this, the sea floor is much deeper, and it gets too cold and dark for corals to live. So at the edge of the reef, there's just the big mysterious sea…

The Tank Gang

When Nemo wakes up in a dentist's fish tank, he doesn't know what to expect. Certainly not the group of stir-crazy fish who greet him – the Tank Gang. And every gang needs a mastermind to cook up ingenious plans. Let's meet Gill, and some of the wacky characters who live at 42 Wallaby Way, Sydney.

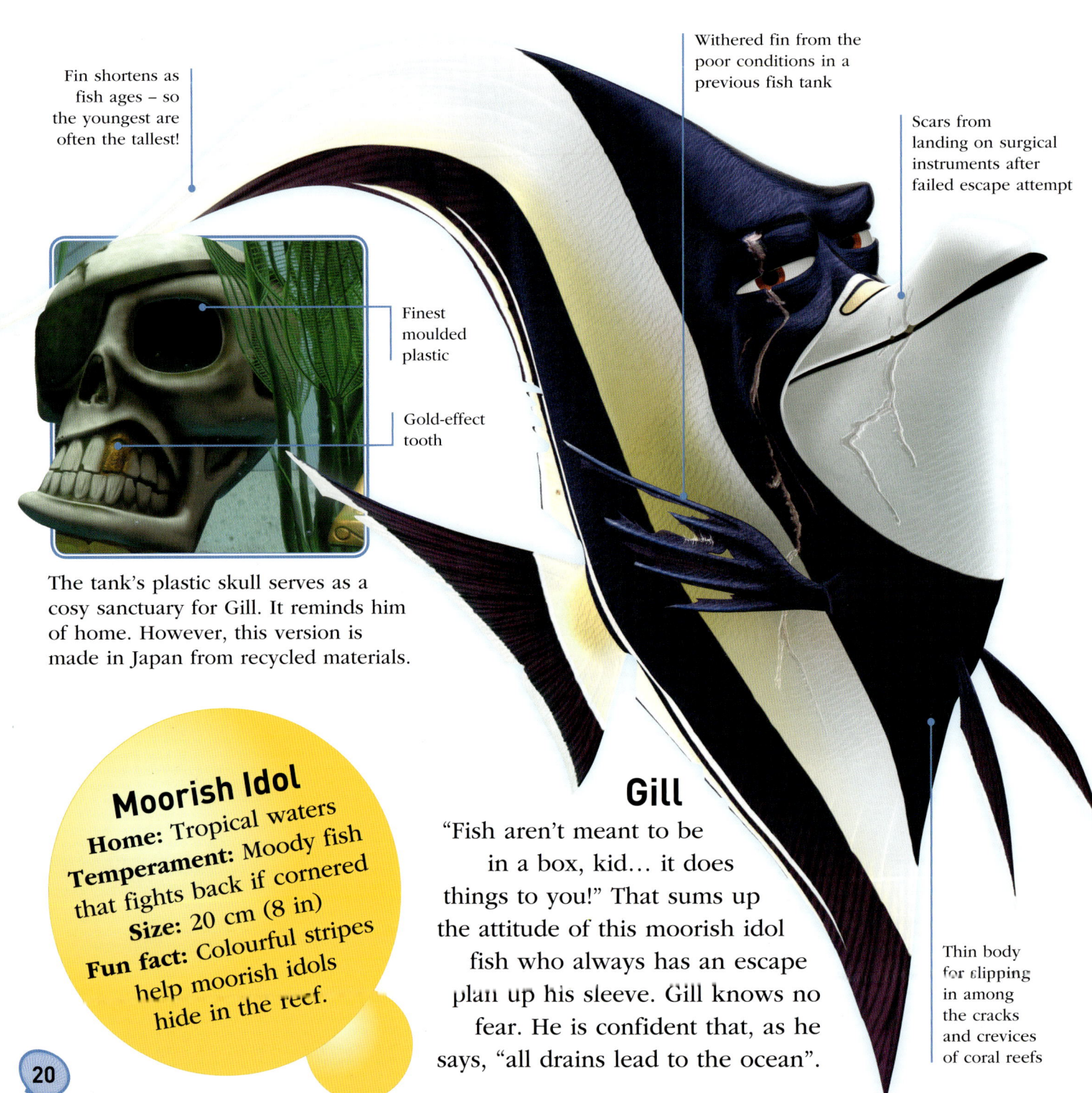

Fin shortens as fish ages – so the youngest are often the tallest!

Withered fin from the poor conditions in a previous fish tank

Scars from landing on surgical instruments after failed escape attempt

Finest moulded plastic

Gold-effect tooth

The tank's plastic skull serves as a cosy sanctuary for Gill. It reminds him of home. However, this version is made in Japan from recycled materials.

Thin body for slipping in among the cracks and crevices of coral reefs

Moorish Idol
Home: Tropical waters
Temperament: Moody fish that fights back if cornered
Size: 20 cm (8 in)
Fun fact: Colourful stripes help moorish idols hide in the reef.

Gill
"Fish aren't meant to be in a box, kid… it does things to you!" That sums up the attitude of this moorish idol fish who always has an escape plan up his sleeve. Gill knows no fear. He is confident that, as he says, "all drains lead to the ocean".

Humbug
Home: Tropical waters
Temperament: Peaceful
Size: 8 cm (3 in)

Deb

Deb is a black and white humbug who loves her own reflection – not that she's vain, she just thinks it's her identical sister, Flo. A reflection follows you around loyally, and when you're feeling low, it does too!

Deb's reflection (but don't tell her!)

Jacques spends many hours hanging out in the tank's diving helmet. It makes him feel like a deep-sea explorer.

Cleaner Shrimp
Size: 5 cm (2 in)
Fact: Cleaner shrimp "clean" fish by eating tiny animals off them!

Jacques

Jacques is a cleaner shrimp. He was once the official cleaner of the President of France's fish tank. When Jacques retired, he was given as a gift to the Prime Minister of Australia, who in turn gave Jacques to his dentist.

Gill's Past

• Gill was a carefree reef-rat as a kid. He fell in with a gang of adventurous fish who set out to see if they could swim around the world before dinner. Guess what – they got hungry and came right back home.

• It was on one of these outings that Gill and his mates were captured and ended up in a pet store. One by one, his friends accepted their fate. But Gill refused to be tamed, and believes that, like Nemo, he can get back his freedom by returning to the ocean, his home and his family.

More Gang!

Ever thought how dull it would be to be stuck in a fish tank all day? Well, think again – being part of this kooky crowd makes captivity almost seem fun… but the one thing that keeps them all going is the eternal hope of escape. Well, that and placing bets on how many fillings each customer is going to need!

Blowfish
Home: Tropical waters
Size: 50 cm (20 in) long
Temperament: Big personalities
Fact: In Japan, blowfish are a delicacy, despite being poisonous. About 100 diners die each year!

Spines point outward at right angles to his body, so Bloat doesn't pop himself!

Bloat

Bloat is a short-tempered blowfish. He looks just like a regular fish until he gets riled, and then he literally blows up with rage! When Bloat was little, his big brother used to bat him around like a volleyball and that just made him angrier. Blowfish are one of nature's most amazing creations, but Bloat doesn't have an inflated view of himself!

Fins used for flapping

Bloat looks a lot less alarming when he is deflated. Blowfish use their blowing-up gimmick to scare off undersea bullies.

Inflation is possible because of elastic skin and no ribs

Spines are poisonous

The tank's treasure chest unleashes bubbles at a rate of 100 per second.

Bubbles

Bubbles likes to chase bubbles. That's why he's named Bubbles. The source of Bubbles' bubbles is a treasure chest at the bottom of the fish tank. Bubbles rarely catches any bubbles.

Yellow Tang
Size: 20 cm (8 in)
Behaviour: Dart about at great speed!

Wide mouth for enjoying Uncle Andy's Dried Mealworms

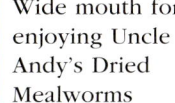

Neurotic fin-in-mouth gesture

Starfish
Home: Sea floors
Fact: If a starfish's arm is cut off, it will grow back again within a year!

Suckers grab hold of surfaces

Peach

Peach is a starfish who clings to the tank wall all day long. She enjoys counting how many coffees the dentist has had and predicting his next toilet break.

Royal gramma fish are known for their rainbow colours.

Gurgle

Gurgle grew up in a crummy pet shop. His tank was choked with slime. In fact, he thought he was green until the day he was put in a plastic bag for delivery to another tank, and the gunk was washed off. Now he's sworn never to be dirty again!

Royal Gramma
Home: Coral reefs
Size: 7 cm (3 in) long
Temperament: Like their own space

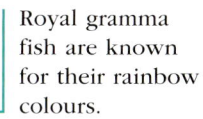

After Nemo is initiated into the tank's club and given the nickname "Shark Bait", Gill explains that he is the key player in their escape plan. Is Nemo up for the task?

Tank Life

To outsiders, it's just a fish tank in dentist Philip P. Sherman's office. But to Gill and the gang, it's home. With its bubbling electric volcano, Polynesian village and plastic gravel, it's a strange place to live – with some very bizarre rules and rituals…

The fish sometimes use pebbles to bet on a patient's diagnosis.

Tiki heads were found in a discount bin at Bob's Fish Mart

Dental Diagnostics

To the gang, dentistry is a serious spectator sport. They have learned all the jargon and can spot a tricky molar extraction diagnosis from X-rays at over 10 metres. Peach is the real dentistry expert. She hopes that one day she'll be called on to spring into action and finish a root canal that the dentist can't handle.

Aqua Scum 2003 ® AS2K3 ®

- Auto filtration compartment
- World wide web communication housing
- Nanotech filtration system
- Fluid dynamic intake grill
- Hyper accelerated robotic pump
- Ourified fluid expulsion grill
- Digital mainframe
- Solar power generator
- Scan data storage motherboard
- The "LASER" primary sensory device

The Aqua Scum 2003

- Gill's plan is to jam the gears of the tank's filter system with a pebble. With the filter broken, the water will get dirty. Then, when the tank is cleaned manually, the fish will be put into plastic bags and they can roll out the window to freedom.

- This ingenious plan fails when the Aqua Scum 2003 is installed. It's an all-purpose, self-cleaning, maintenance-free, salt-water purifier.

- This device laser-scans the tank every five minutes, so it will never become dirty again! Gill's master plan is ruined… but on the bright side, the water does feel kind of softer on the scales.

The tank sits in the wall between the lobby and the exam room. The fish hold secret meetings at the volcano they call Mt. Wannahockaloogie. It is here that Nemo swims through the ring of fire (actually a stream of bubbles) to join the gang! "Ah-hoo-wah-hee. Ah-ho-ho-ho!"

Mount Wannahockaloogie adorns the lobby side of the tank.

pH-balanced saltwater

Fake coral remind the fish of home

Chuckles used to spy on the dentist from the ship's crow's nest.

Tank Ship

The tank's pirate ship faces the exam room. The fish usually avoid the ship because it reminds them of their old pal, Chuckles, who was a present for the dentist's niece, Darla, last year. Unfortunately, Darla shook the bag too hard and Chuckles went belly up. The tank gang tried to lower the flag to half-mast, but sadly it doesn't move.

Dentist's Lobby

With its sailing-theme wallpaper and hanging life preservers, Philip Sherman's lobby says a lot about the man. For Philip Sherman, dentistry is a way to support his true love: scuba diving! He would prefer a deep-sea dive to a molar extraction any day. However, Phil continues the family line of Sherman dentists. His great-great-grandfather opened the practice on Wallaby Way in 1895.

P. Sherman graduated second from last in his class, but the awards on his wall tell a different story.

- Buzz Lightyear action figure
- Darla's drawings
- M is for Monster book
- Fish tank in specially built hatch

Lobby Life

P. Sherman is known as a family dentist. When he took over the practice from his father, he redecorated the lobby to appeal to patients of all ages... and his sea-going interests. With a fish tank, toys and plenty of reading material, there is something to please everyone.

The Diving Dentist

• Dr. Sherman often goes diving with his old chums from dental school at Alice Springs University. They call him "Skip" – since he had a lucky skipper cap he would wear during exams.

• Philip Sherman is the captain of his dive boat, The Aussie Flosser. He hopes to sail around the world when he retires from dentistry.

• Pet peeve: having to buy sugar-free products all the time in case he bumps into another dentist in the supermarket.

Face mask – always label clearly with your name and address!

Luminous stripes make Dr. Sherman look slimmer

Philip Sherman never takes fish from the reef except when he finds one "struggling for life" with an injured fin.

Luxury brace set, received at special discount

Chuckles

Overalls stained with brown milk after accident with bowl of Chock-O's sugar-coated caramel cube cereal

P. Sherman's appointments calendar

Darla

Darla Sherman is a pupil at Waltzing Matilda Primary School in Sydney. She loves fish and always shakes the bag with excitement when she gets one. However, she thinks her uncle has very sleepy fish. Maybe the silly gas gets to them, too?

Lucky Darla always gets a free checkup from her uncle on her birthday... and a present. Last year, after Darla's fishy present died, her uncle bought her now-favourite sweatshirt which says "Rock 'n' Roll Girl".

Exam Room

Here it is – Philip Sherman's exam room, where all the action takes place. Many famous patients have come through the doors of this room for a painless root canal or cavity filling. It is a good thing that the fish in the tank can't talk!

With no wife or kids to lavish gifts upon, Dr. Sherman pours all his money into toys, whether it's an ocean-going dive boat, the latest Deluxe Relax-o-matic Dental Activity Facilitator (that's the chair) or just a brand-new pair of really sharp tools.

High-tech oral implement

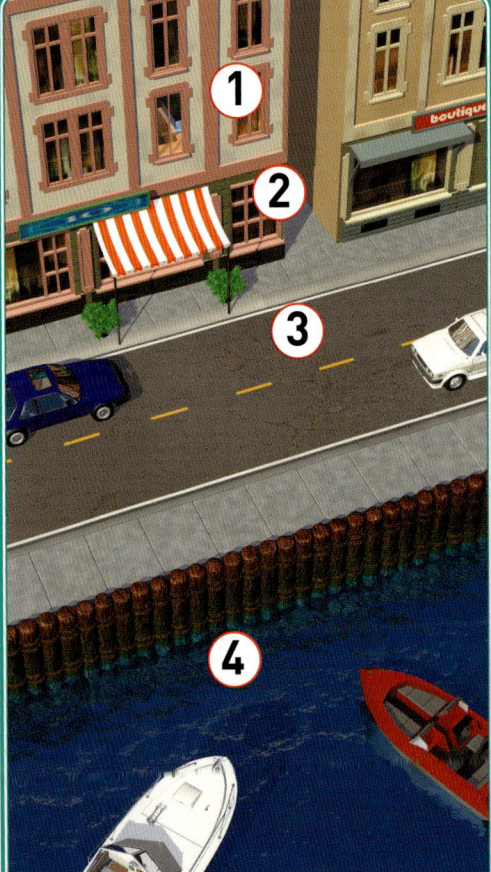

Your Mission

Should you wish to accept, your instructions for escape are detailed below. Good luck, fish.
1. Once in your plastic bag, roll across the counter to the ledge and out the window. (Make sure the window is open before attempting.)
2. Aim for the awning to cushion the drop.
3. At the street, look both ways before bag-rolling.
4. Bounce over the pilings and into the harbour to the big blue!
Mission accomplished!

The fish tank – patients like to have something to fix their attention on when they are "in the chair"

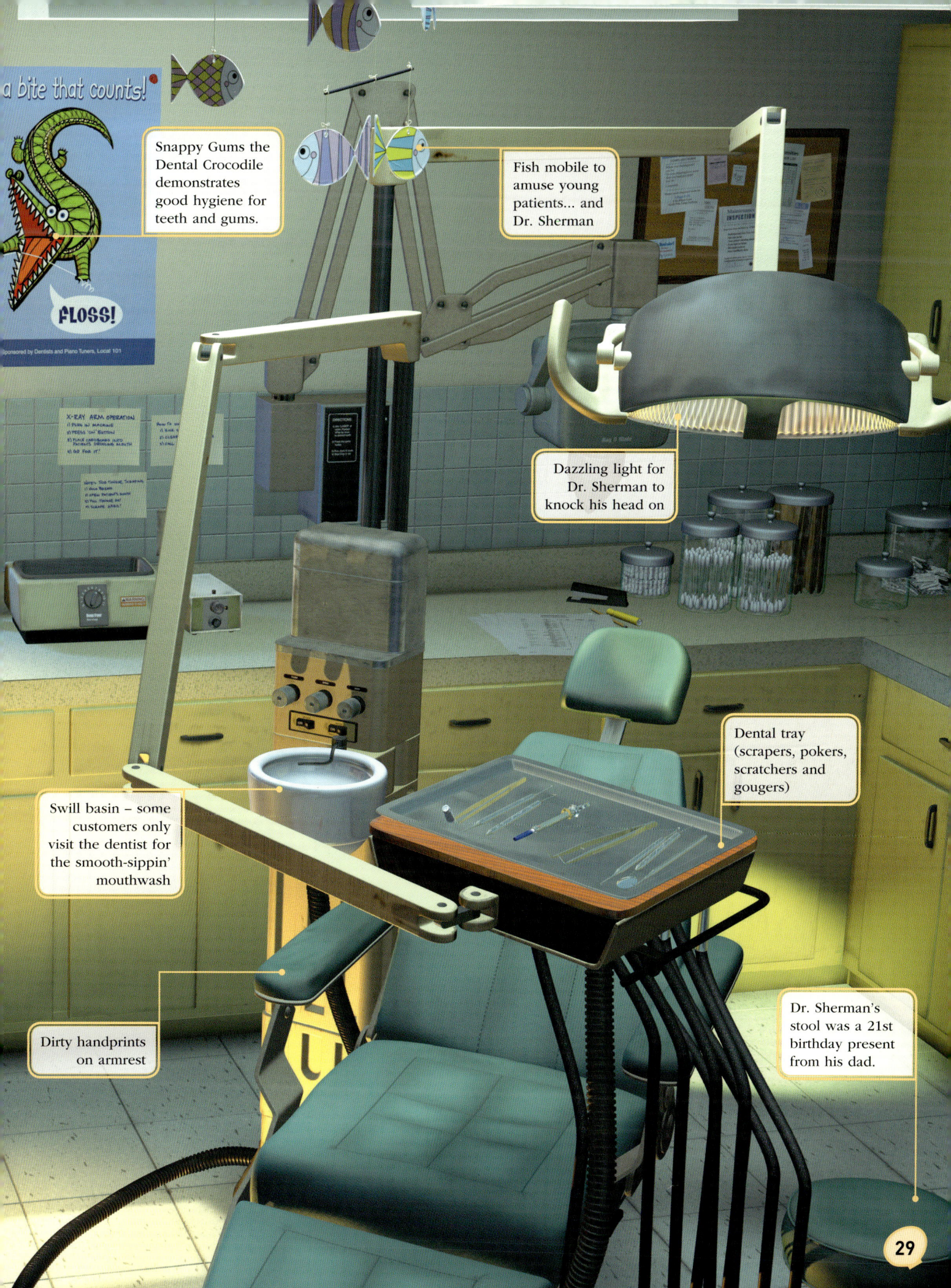

Bruce

G'day mate! The lovable guy with the chainsaw smile is Bruce, a great white shark born and raised on the Great Barrier Reef. He looks like a real terror of the deep, but appearances can be deceiving – Bruce is a shark with a crusade! He has created a vegetarian group, because he wants to change the bad image sharks have for chewing up just about everyone they meet. His slogan is "fish are friends… not food!"

Bruce is a persuasive public speaker at his anti-meat-eating meetings. Despite ravenously chasing Marlin and Dory, he will always consider them members of his group. If they get into any future scrapes, they'll have a cool buddy to call on!

Tail is used for steering, moving and speed control

Great White
Home: Warm waters
Size: About 4 m (13 ft) long
Favourite food: Bruce thrives on vegetarian kelp salad but most sharks eat fish.
Fact: Great whites have 3,000 teeth!

Body built like a torpedo for speed

Friends For Life

When Bruce meets Marlin and Dory, he is keen to make a good impression – not eating them is a good start. He invites them to his next party, which is held in a sunken submarine.

Sharks' trademark – the triangular dorsal fin

Sharks can't help staring – their eyelids do not blink

Body bears the scars of many previous run-ins with natural enemies

You may wonder why the sharks' meeting place remains undisturbed by nosy humans. Well, those aren't party balloons floating outside – they're unexploded mines. Wonder what would happen if something disturbed them…?

Nostrils sniff out prey

Typical inward curving teeth of a serious hunter – once bitten, it's hard to get unhooked

Shark Bites

- Bruce never knew his father, who was always out chasing after surfers, and biting cruise ships. His need for company inspired him to form his vegetarian lifestyle group.

- As a kid, sensitive Bruce didn't understand why humans avoided him. "What, did somebody make a movie about a bad shark or something?" he sometimes wondered.

Anchor & Chum

Bruce, Anchor and Chum met at a feeding frenzy. Being good guys deep down, they felt racked with guilt at pigging out on so many of their finny brethren, and decided to form a vegetarian shark society. They take it in turns to bring snacks to their weekly meetings. Sushi is frowned upon, but a nice seaweed sandwich keeps them satisfied.

Today's meeting is Step Five: Bring a Fish Friend. Chum, unfortunately, seems to have misplaced his friend.

Anchor

This happy hammerhead is self-conscious about the irregular shape of his head, and appreciates his mates not teasing him about it. He always avoids swimming with swordfish and spiral-toothed narwal, because he thinks that together they'll look like an underwater toolbox.

Super hearing – hammerheads can even hear air-bubbles moving through the water (so be careful what you eat before diving!)

Experts are still not 100% sure, but they think the wide-apart eyes and nostrils help the shark detect prey with pinpoint accuracy.

Each tooth is jagged, making it quite unreasonably sharp.

Hammerheads use their tailfins to twist and turn.

Big belly

Hammerhead
Home: Warm waters
Size: 3.5 m (1.5 ft) long
Shark fact: Like to have "fun" with stingrays by pinning them down with their hammerheads and "playfully" nipping their wings!

The highlight of any club meeting is the chance to offer up your testimonial and tell your fish brothers about your problems. Remember, you are a nice shark, not a mindless eating machine.

The sharks are keen to show their enthusiasm for the fish-free diet, none more so than Anchor. He loves giving things up, and even tried to give up swimming once! But since sharks need to swim to breathe, this idea didn't last long.

Bite Size Facts

- Sharks suffer from a serial-killer image in the human world. In fact, they are much less vicious toward us than you might think. Some experts think sharks only attack people because they mistake them for seals or dolphins, which it is easy to do when you're hungry.

- The toughest part of being in the group is when one of your buddies loses control. Then it's your job to intervene and keep him on track with the programme. You should also apologise profusely to the fish your friend is trying to eat.

- Blenny is a new guest at the sharks' fish-friendly meetings. Anchor befriended him against his will during a new recruitment drive.

Blenny is still overcoming his fear of sharks.

Blenny

Chum

Secretly something of an upper-class shark, Chum is a mako who likes to hang with Bruce and Anchor. He puts on a rough-sounding accent he learned from a caretaker at his posh predator boarding school. Chum worries he'll be spotted one day by his hoity-toity friends, fraternizing with the local reef-raff.

Mako Shark
Home: Warm waters
Character: Unpredictable
Size: 2.4 m (8 ft) long
Top speed: 35 kph (22 mph)
Hobbies: Stalking dolphins (who think they're so cute)

Dark eyes allow Chum to look smarter than he really is

Souvenir of a recent tussle with a fisherman (Chum won)

Huge, curved teeth – Chum's pals often call him "old snaggletooth" (but not to his face, of course)

Dapper white underside sets off the dark grey-blue top well

Makos pride themselves on having the sleekest bodies of all sharks.

Sunken Sub

Lying on the ocean floor, the submarine is a relic of an old sea battle. Its once shining corridors are now rusted, and have become a battleground in the fight against eating fish. The sharks meet here to battle their hunger for fish and change their bad image. To do this, they must first change themselves.

They cram just about everything into a sub, including the kitchen sink – and here it is.

The sharks hold meetings in the sub's dining room, known as the mess hall. Actually the whole sub is a bit of a mess, but that's another story. We've taken the liberty of adding another hole in the ship to show you Marlin and Dory's race through the sub from the hungry Bruce.

The mess hall – bring a friend!

Underwater Hang-out

- The submarine was lost during World War II. It went down in heavily mined waters, but suffered surprisingly little damage.

- The sharks have been using this wreck as a hang-out for years. But it is about to be relocated… by a massive explosion. When Dory and Marlin needed a safe place to hide from Bruce, maybe a torpedo tube wasn't the best idea ever…

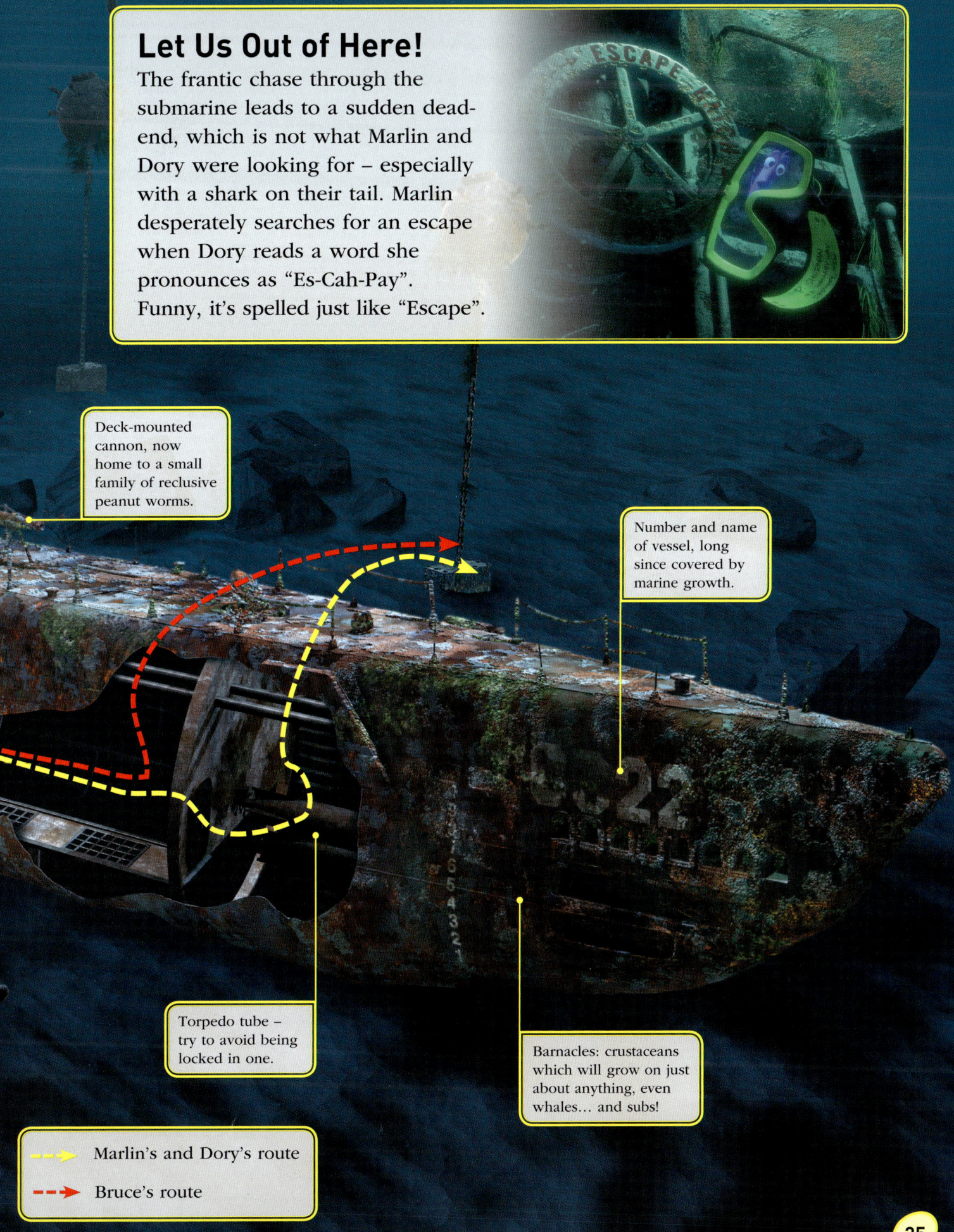

Let Us Out of Here!

The frantic chase through the submarine leads to a sudden dead-end, which is not what Marlin and Dory were looking for – especially with a shark on their tail. Marlin desperately searches for an escape when Dory reads a word she pronounces as "Es-Cah-Pay". Funny, it's spelled just like "Escape".

Deck-mounted cannon, now home to a small family of reclusive peanut worms.

Number and name of vessel, long since covered by marine growth.

Torpedo tube – try to avoid being locked in one.

Barnacles: crustaceans which will grow on just about anything, even whales… and subs!

- - → Marlin's and Dory's route
- - → Bruce's route

35

The Abyss

Welcome to the place where it's always night! At the bottom of the ocean, there's no light – just a cold, inky blackness filled with creatures that are the stuff of nightmares. The trouble is, these nightmares are real! The abyss dwellers are delighted to see anyone that ventures down from the seas above… because it's always nice to have a midnight snack.

Anglerfish use an elongated spine as a fishing rod.

Dark body stays hidden in the darkness

Small eyes, as there is usually nothing to see in the abyss, and never anything good on TV

Millions of glowing bacteria live inside the "lure", creating a lightbulb effect.

Teeth curve inwards to ease prey in, and prevent a swift exit

Fearsome Depths

When Marlin and Dory swim into the darkness of the abyss searching for the diver's mask that could lead them to Nemo, Dory becomes disoriented. She thinks Marlin's voice is her conscience. It's a creepy place that plays tricks on your mind – like seeing ghostly lights…

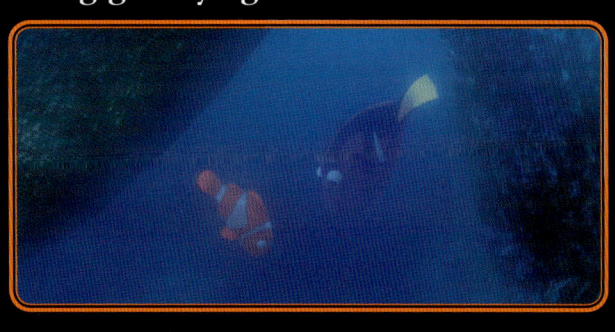

Anglerfish Facts

- Anglerfish make their living not by means of speed or power, but by a clever gimmick. Rather than chasing after a fish, they dangle a lantern in front of their heads to lure it near to their mouth. Then they gobble up the mesmerized creature!

- In the anglerfish world, the female rules. She grows nearly 20 times bigger than the male and does all the hunting – only females have glowing lures. Puny males rely on her for everything – food, security, setting the TV…

A friendly light seems to call to you, inviting you to come and bask in its glow. Down in that murk, it's the most welcome sight you've ever seen. You want to get closer and reach out to it. SNAP! You just got caught by the fisherman of the abyss. He's the deep-sea anglerfish, and you took the bait!

Stomach can stretch to fit in extra-big dinners

Anglerfish
Home: At the darkest and scariest depths of the ocean
Size: (females) 1.2 m (4 ft) (males) 6.3 cm (2.5 in)
Temperament: Anglerfish are eating machines – not fun-loving at all!

Trapped

Marlin didn't take "Escaping an Anglerfish lessons" in school, but he still manages to trap the anglerfish with a diver's mask. He finally learns what the mask says, but the more immediate lesson is: never taunt anglerfish!

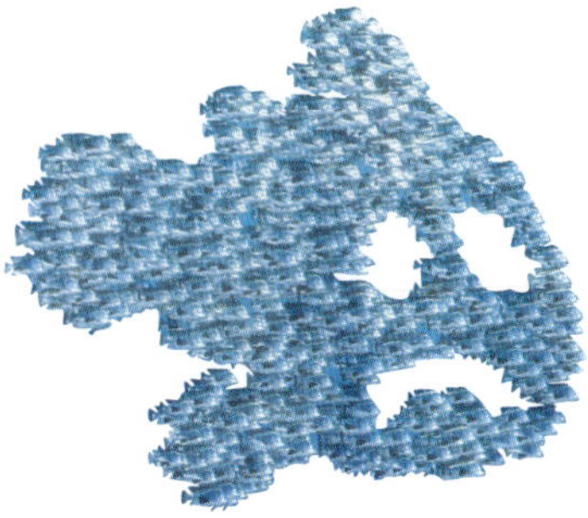

Moonfish

No other crowd of fish enjoy hanging out together like moonfish. They are the impersonators of the sea, using their talents to amuse their friends and frighten their enemies. They once scared off a barracuda by creating the likeness of a hammerhead shark. This was great until they got invited to a feeding frenzy by a bunch of *real* hammerheads!

Marlin tells Dory he wants to finish the journey on his own, which upsets her. Fortunately, when the moonfish swim by to ask her what's wrong, Dory has already forgotten why she was crying.

With no predators around, the moonfish use their talents to entertain other fish! Each year they put on a show, "Oh Neptune!", which makes even the frowniest mollusc smile.

Impressionists

• These guys' slick routine is the result of endless practise. Giving directions is easy, but becoming an arrow to point the way is hard work.

• You want difficult? Then how about this… the moonfish do an impression of the Sydney Opera House.

• These jokers give Marlin a hard time at first because he's a clownfish. Moonfish work on their comedy hard, and are jealous of a clownfish's natural talent for being funny. Lucky Marlin didn't tell any jokes and spoil the illusion…

Moonfish
Home: Warm waters
Temperament: Social
Fishy fact: Moonfish have a peculiar habit of lying out flat on the water surface like circular moons, hence their name!

Big eye for seeing what the others are doing

Scales reflect light and look like they are glowing

Helping Out

At first, the moonfish play games with Marlin, making him realize what a grumpy-gills he can be sometimes. However, once the moonfish learn of Marlin and Dory's quest to find Nemo they're happy to help. They even use their talents to warn Dory to go through the big trench up ahead, not over it. Good call! Now if only she can remember their advice…

Jellyfish

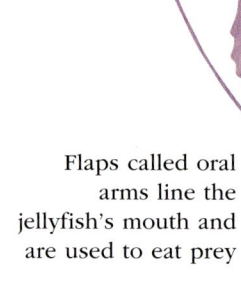

They look like mindless blobs of jelly, meandering aimlessly through the ocean. But rumour has it that jellyfish are really the most intelligent creatures in the sea. It is claimed they spend all day stumping each other with complicated maths problems and riddles!

Round umbrella-like body moves the animals with a pumping motion

Flaps called oral arms line the jellyfish's mouth and are used to eat prey

Bad Squishy!
When Dory comes across a baby jellyfish, she calls the little cutie "Squishy" and wants to claim it has her own – until it stings her! Immune to its stings, Marlin shoos the baby away, unaware that jelly mums and dads are about to surround them.

Jellyfish Trench

• Nice Trench. When Dory and Marlin reach the jellyfish trench, Dory has a feeling that they should swim through it, but she cannot remember why. Unfortunately, Marlin distracts her and they swim over the trench into the jellyfish forest.

• Jellyfish are very proud of their tentacles. They grow them as long as they can, and hate having a bad tentacle day!

• Clownfish joke: How do you make a jellyfish laugh? Answer: Give him ten tickles (tentacles)!

Long tentacles are covered in stingers to stun prey

Making Friends

Dory thinks that jellyfish are fun. To her, they are big, gelatinous swimming trampolines. She is just too forgetful for her own good, and Marlin has to think fast if they're going to escape from the jelly-jam.

Jellies have long stinging tentacles that can stun their prey. And if the two fish friends don't escape quickly, they've had their chips!

Jellyfish
Home: Oceans worldwide
Size: up to 2.4 m (8 ft) across
Most dangerous: Australia's box jellyfish can kill a person!
Fact: Jellyfish are not fish, but are related to sea anemones.

How do you escape from a great slobbery mass of jellyfish? The trick is to bounce on their tops, because their blobby heads don't sting. See, it always pays to use your head – or someone else's!

Turtles

Surfing the ocean currents, turtles are the coolest dudes in the sea. They love to swim, bask in the sun and ride the waves. But turtles are tough guys, too. Their shells can survive the battering of stormy seas, and they can live to incredible ages. Nemo has always wanted to know exactly how long they live. Marlin is lucky enough to meet one who is 150 years old, and still young.

Turtles
Animal group: Reptiles
Home: Oceans worldwide
Size: up to 2 m (6.5 ft)
Temperament: Laid-back
Fun fact: Turtles breathe air using little nostrils on their heads.

Crush
A hippie turtle, Crush first decided to settle down and have kids at the super-young age (for a turtle) of 57. He is dedicated to the lifelong pursuit of riding the perfect current. He loves teaching his little dudes to surf the gnarly currents of life without wiping out.

Little dudes listen wide-eyed to Marlin's story

Back flippers are for steering

Shell is a streamlined shape to slice through the water, which means greater cruising speed

Turtle Eyes
- Turtles are attracted to bright lights. When they are born on a beach, the babies sometimes mistakenly head toward street or house lights, instead of the sea.
- Tears sometimes drop from turtles' eyes, but it doesn't mean they're unhappy. They just drink a lot of salty sea water and have to drain out the salt through their eyes.

Squirt

Crush's son, Squirt, learned to surf the waves at an early age. Like all turtles, he was born on a beach and had to make his way back to his parents in the sea, braving hungry crabs and snapping seagulls. Now he knows no fear!

Squirt's favourite food is yummy seaweed.

Worn out from escaping the jellyfish, Marlin and Dory might have ended up nowhere if Crush hadn't guided them into the E.A.C. – the East Australian Current. It's like an express highway through the ocean and ends up in the waters close to Sydney.

Strong beak for shredding seaweed to snack-size bites and snacking on the odd tough-skinned strawberry jellyfish

Strong front flippers beat the water almost like wings

Goodbye Dudes

Waterways can get a bit congested and the E.A.C. is no exception. Hundreds of turtles and sea creatures ride the E.A.C. for miles to reach their next destination. When exiting the current to Sydney, one must always follow proper exiting technique. Remember: rip it, roll it and punch it.

The Whale

When Marlin and Dory are in need of directions to Sydney, Dory spots someone she can ask. Under the sea, distances can be deceptive... the "little fella" that she calls out to turns out to be the biggest living creature in the whole ocean – the blue whale!

Blue whale
Home: Oceans worldwide
Animal group: Mammal (same as humans!)
Size: 24 m (80 ft) long
Comments: Whales can talk to each other over hundreds of miles of ocean.

Whale Song

Attracting a whale's attention is never easy, and not always a good idea if you're a krill with career plans. But Dory's whale song does the trick – despite sounding like an upset stomach!

Long, thin flippers can be 2.4 metres (8 feet) long

Big mouth swallows up to 40 million krill (tiny shrimps) a day!

Pleated grooves allow throat to expand during feeding

Inspection

Has the whale heard the story of Marlin and his quest to find Nemo? Maybe so, as whales have a way of picking up gossip from hundreds of kilometres away, in their extraordinary songs. While our heroes are debating their next move, the kindly leviathan cruises up and checks out his future passengers.

In the Whale

After Marlin is swallowed up by the whale, he thinks he will never get to tell Nemo how old sea turtles are, but Dory remains optimistic. She convinces Marlin that everything is going to be alright… and it is! The whale shoots them out of his blowhole and into Sydney Harbour.

Whales are big enough to swallow tugboats. But they feed on one of the tiniest creatures of the sea: krill. They strain them out of the water through their baleen, the special plates inside their mouths.

Shell helps crabs survive stormy waters and protects their insides

Skeleton is on the outside of body

Powerful claws for holding food… and tearing wrappers off candy bars!

Bernie

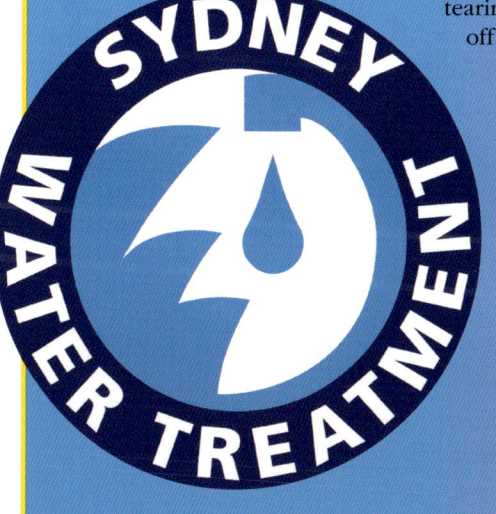

Under Sydney Harbour

• The Sydney Water Treatment plant is a high-tech, environmentally sound facility that processes the waste water from Sydney's homes and businesses.

• Every day, its outlet pipes release treated water into the sea. The plant is highly successful at cleaning up Sydney's wastewater, but a few hearty chunks of food, plant matter, bits of candy bar and fish from P. Sherman's office do make it through.

• To crabs like Bernie and his pal, Baz, an outlet pipe is like a magical, never-ending, all-you-can-eat salad bar! Bernie and Baz steadfastly guard their section of the pipe, which is the best they've found in years. No wonder they only stop eating to say "Ah, sweet nectar of life".

Sydney Harbour

This is a cool place to visit if you're a human tourist, but Sydney Harbour is one mean neighbourhood for a fish. If the greedy gulls don't get you, then the peckish pelicans will! When Marlin arrives at the last stage of his quest to find Nemo, he knows that reaching his son will be no picnic. If he's not careful, he'll end up as one himself!

Is that a school of moonfish practising their impressions? No, it's the *real* Sydney Opera House!

Harbour

Sydney Harbour teems with fishing boats, ferries, cruise ships and sailing boats. Overlooking the harbour is Sydney Harbour Bridge, known to locals as the "Coat Hanger". Dr. Sherman's boat, The Aussie Flosser, is moored somewhere. Will Marlin and Dory be able to find it?

Nigel the Pelican

Nigel was hatched in a nest atop Dr. Sherman's office. At a young age, he wondered what happened to humans when they went inside. The minute he learned to fly, he perched at the window of the exam room to take a look. He has since become a dental expert, and discusses Phil Sherman's technique with the fish-tank occupants.

Sydney Life

• It isn't just the seagulls who are competitive in Sydney – the human population is very inventive at making a living, too. Check out some of their business cards…

• Wallaby Way is famous for its dentist practices and its shops selling sweets – somehow the two seem to encourage each other.

• Sydney Harbour is the deepest natural harbour in the world – that's why the whale who carried Nemo and Dory was able to get so close.

CAT & DOG DENTISTRY
Dr. Smiley Teeth, DDS, Vet.
44 Wallaby Way, Sydney, Australia

SUGAR CANDY
Specializing in Gooey-Stick-to-Your-Teeth Goodness
41 Wallaby Way, Sydney, Australia

"Don't forget to panic!"

Underwater Scuba Dentistry
40 Wallaby Way, Sydney, Australia

Nigel tried to get the other pelicans interested in dentistry, but all they wanted to do was sit on top of the local bait shop and talk about how stupid seagulls were.

Tough gullet for swallowing just about anything

Webbed feet – great for catching crumbs

Hop inside my mouth if you want to live! Nigel makes Marlin an offer he can't refuse, as he takes him to find his son.

Seagulls

"Mine! Mine! Mine!" That's the cry you'll hear from the gulls down at the harbour. Each scavenger has only one goal: get what's mine and get it now! This has earned the seagulls a bad reputation with pelicans, who think they are truly rats with wings.

DEEP SEA STICKERS

How to use the stickers

1. Read the captions and, using the labels beside each sticker, choose the image that best fits in the space available.

2. Don't forget that your stickers can be stuck down and peeled off again. If you are careful, you can use your Finding Nemo stickers more than once.

3. You can also use your Finding Nemo stickers to decorate your own books.

On The Reef

Nemo's adventures start on his first day of school. Angry at his father, he swims beyond the safety of the reef and is captured by a scuba diver. Now Marlin, Nemo's father, must set out on an epic adventure into the open ocean to find his missing son.

Bad Comedian
Marlin is the middle child of 103 brothers and sisters. He is always trying to tell jokes, but, for a clownfish, he is not that funny.

Father and Son
Marlin has been overprotective of Nemo since his family was attacked by a barracuda.

Forgetful Fish
Dory was born with a bad memory. It runs in her family. At least she thinks it does. She doesn't remember.

Coral Home
Nemo lives with his dad in a quiet corner of the coral reef.

Record-breaking Reef
Nemo's home, the Great Barrier Reef in Australia, is the largest structure in the world made by living things.

Little Fish
Nemo is a six-year-old clownfish. He's eager to explore the wonders of the ocean.

Horse Play
Sheldon, a kid seahorse, likes to gallop around the reef with his pals. Water makes him sneeze, and he uses kelp tissues, which he finds awfully slimy.

Octopus Friend
Pearl is an octopus with eight tentacles (one is slightly shorter than the rest). She spurts ink when frightened.

Mischief-maker
Tad is a long-nosed butterfly fish who likes to have fun and cause trouble. Because he's so smart, he gets bored easily. Once he got in trouble for hiding all his teacher's coral chalk.

Colourful Coral
Over 350 kinds of coral live on the Great Barrier Reef. There are many different colours and shapes.

Living Coral
Though colourful coral branches look like plants, they are actually made of thousands of tiny animals called polyps!

Big Fin, Little Fin
Nemo's small fin makes him swim awkwardly, but he will never let it slow him down.

New Friends
Dory is a kind-hearted soul. She loves to help others, like her new friend Marlin.

Serious Parent
Nemo's father, Marlin, takes his responsibilities as a parent seriously indeed. Such seriousness is quite unusual in a clownfish.

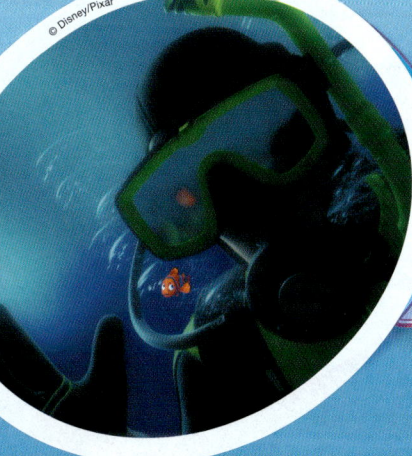

Fishnapped!
Dentist Philip Sherman lives to explore the mystery and majesty of the Great Barrier Reef, and the human mouth!

Smart Fish
Dory is very educated. She can read human, speak whale and understand 42 different fish dialects.

Class Act
Before meeting Marlin, Dory graduated first in her class at fish school, and was meant to give a speech. But she forgot.

Tank Life

After his capture, Nemo finds himself in a dentist's office fish tank in Sydney, Australia. He soon makes friends with the other stir-crazy tank fish, who really should get out more – if only they could!

Mucky Fish
Gurgle grew up in a filthy tank in a pet store. He used to think he was a green fish, but it was just a coating of slime!

Determined Loner
Gill is a scarred moorish idol fish who is determined to make an escape from the tank.

Temper Tantrum
Bloat unpredictably inflates with anger when provoked. It all goes back to his childhood. His brother Bob never tired of picking on him.

Sisters
Deb had never had a long-term friend until she met her sister, Flo. Now they do everything together. The fact that Flo is Deb's reflection in the tank glass really shouldn't matter!

Presidential Pet
Jacques is a cleaner shrimp. His favourite pastime is cleaning! He once belonged to the President of France.

Tank Lookout
Stuck on the tank glass, Peach finds comfort in watching the outside world. She's also become the tank's resident dentistry expert.

Escape Plan
All the tank fish have accepted their fate except Gill. He quickly finds a way to use Nemo in his latest escape plan.

Effervescent!
Bubbles likes to chase the bubbles that pop-up from a little plastic treasure chest. His favourite food is Uncle Andy's Dried Mealworms.

Shark Shocks!

Bruce, Anchor and Chum met at a feeding frenzy. Racked with the guilt of eating so many fish, they are trying to stop their rampant appetites. They have decided to have regular meetings to offer support to each other. Will the sharks stick to the vegetarian kelp salad and stay off the sushi?

Frightened Fish
Marlin is not quite sure he wants to attend a "party" with a shark.

Slumming It
Chum is a mako shark from a well-to-do shark family on the North side of the reef. He likes to hang out with the rougher sharks, who his hoity-toity friends call "reef-raff".

Lonesome Shark
Bruce is a great white shark who had a lonely childhood. He hardly knew his father, who was always out chasing surfers and biting cruise ships.

Nervous Marlin
Marlin's encounter with sharks is not one he'd like to repeat. This doesn't stop him from repeating the story to his friends though.

Headache!
Anchor is a hammerhead who is very self-conscious about the shape of his head. He hates anyone staring at it.

Honoured Guests
The shark tells Marlin and Dory that today's meeting is Step Five: Bring a fish friend. After all, "Fish are friends, not food".

Forget Fear!
Dory forgets many things. She even forgets to be scared when greeted by a shark!

Sea Journey

The expansive ocean is full of surprises for Marlin and Dory – not all of them welcome ones! They learn new skills such as how to cross a field of jellyfish by jumping on their tops and why deep-sea anglerfish are best avoided due to their sharp teeth. They also make new friends, including a 150-year-old turtle.

Vital Clue
When Dr. Sherman captures Nemo, he drops his mask. Fortunately for Marlin, the dentist's address is written on it.

Dive Dive
Fish and sharks are always flattered when humans drop presents for them, such as submarines or boats. They make good meeting spaces.

Buddies
Dory is happy to help Marlin look for his son, only she cannot remember his name. Is she looking for Harpo or Elmo?

Team Effort
These fish swim in formation, making shapes to scare off predators or just to get a laugh.

Out of the Deep
The sight of a deep-sea anglerfish wearing a dive mask might be funny to some fish. But not if you're two inches from its razor-sharp fangs.

Ted
Ted was originally from Sydney, where he still has relatives. A born performer, he left to join a school of travelling impersonators.

Dad Problems
On his journey to find Nemo, Marlin confronts his worst fears. In the end, he learns to never give up, to "keep swimming" through an unpredictable world.

Underwater Forest
Jellyfish can form into forests, using their tentacles to paralyse and catch creatures that swim by.

Unfriendly Creatures
Jellyfish seem to be mindless blobs, meandering aimlessly through the deep. Perhaps they're quite intelligent creatures, but they're just too snobby to say hello.

Reunion
Marlin and Nemo reunite in the fishing grounds off Sydney Harbour after their long journey.

Turtle Guides
The turtles guide Marlin and Dory to their exit for Sydney off the East Australian Current.

Learning to Laugh
Dory's enthusiasm for life soon begins to rub off on Marlin. Eventually, he learns to stop worrying so much and enjoy himself more!

Jelly-fright!
Marlin lives in an anemone and is used to stings, but how can he save Dory?

Little Dude
Crush's son, Squirt, is a little surfer dude learning to ride the gnarly ocean currents with his dad. Sweet!

Firm Friends
Dory forgets most things, but she always remembers to stick with Marlin.

Young At Heart
Crush is a laid-back father of 10 who teaches his little dudes to ride the swirly currents of life without wiping out.

Famous Fish!

News travels fast in the ocean, and soon sea creatures everywhere are talking about Marlin's incredible journey to find his son. He has been nicknamed Superfish and rumour has it that even his jokes have become funny.

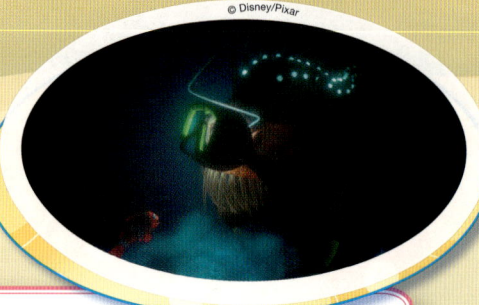

Nemo's Home
Clownfish live in the stinging tentacles of sea anemones.

School Trip
Mr. Ray is everyone's favourite science teacher. He takes the class on field trips singing educational songs along the way.

Horsey Habits
Sheldon's favourite food is lightly salted crustacean puffs.

Eight-legged Facts
Pearl's favourite food is crab cakes with sea cucumber salad. Her hobby is making shell jewellry.

Here Comes Trouble
Tad's favourite hobbies are drawing in the sand, making up cool stories and being obnoxious.

Shark Tip
Bruce has given up eating fish, but don't get a nosebleed around him. He'll revert to his old ways faster than a hurricane.

Nemo the Hero
Nemo learns that he has the bravest dad in the sea. And his dad is pretty proud of him too!

Turtle Games
Dory is young at heart, and enjoys playing hide and seek with the young turtles.

Deep-sea Nightmares
As a child, the anglerfish hated bedtimes, when his parents would call "lights out".

Stickers

Nemo Dory Tad

Coral Marlin Coral

Coral

Coral

Dory

Sheldon A diver captures Nemo

Nemo

Pearl Dory and Marlin

Gurgle

Stickers

Gill and Nemo

Deb

Marlin and Nemo

Marlin and Nemo

Gill

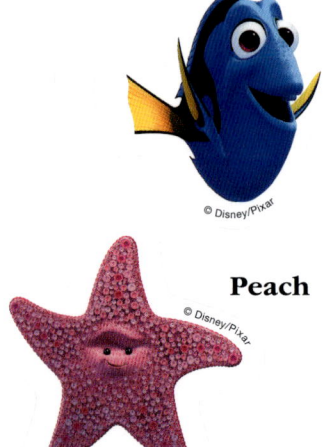

Bubbles

Bloat

Peach

Jacques

Bruce appears

Marlin meets Dory

Anchor

The ocean can be dangerous

Stickers

Sheldon

Chum

Marlin and Dory

Diver's mask

Bruce

Dory and Marlin

School of fish

Jellyfish

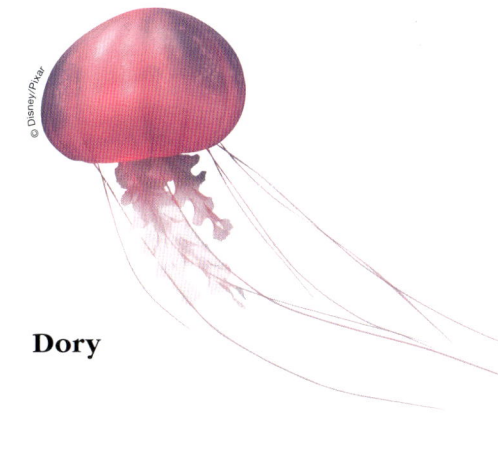

Marlin outsmarts anglerfish

Ted

Dory

Squirt

Nemo and Marlin

Jellyfish sting!

Stickers

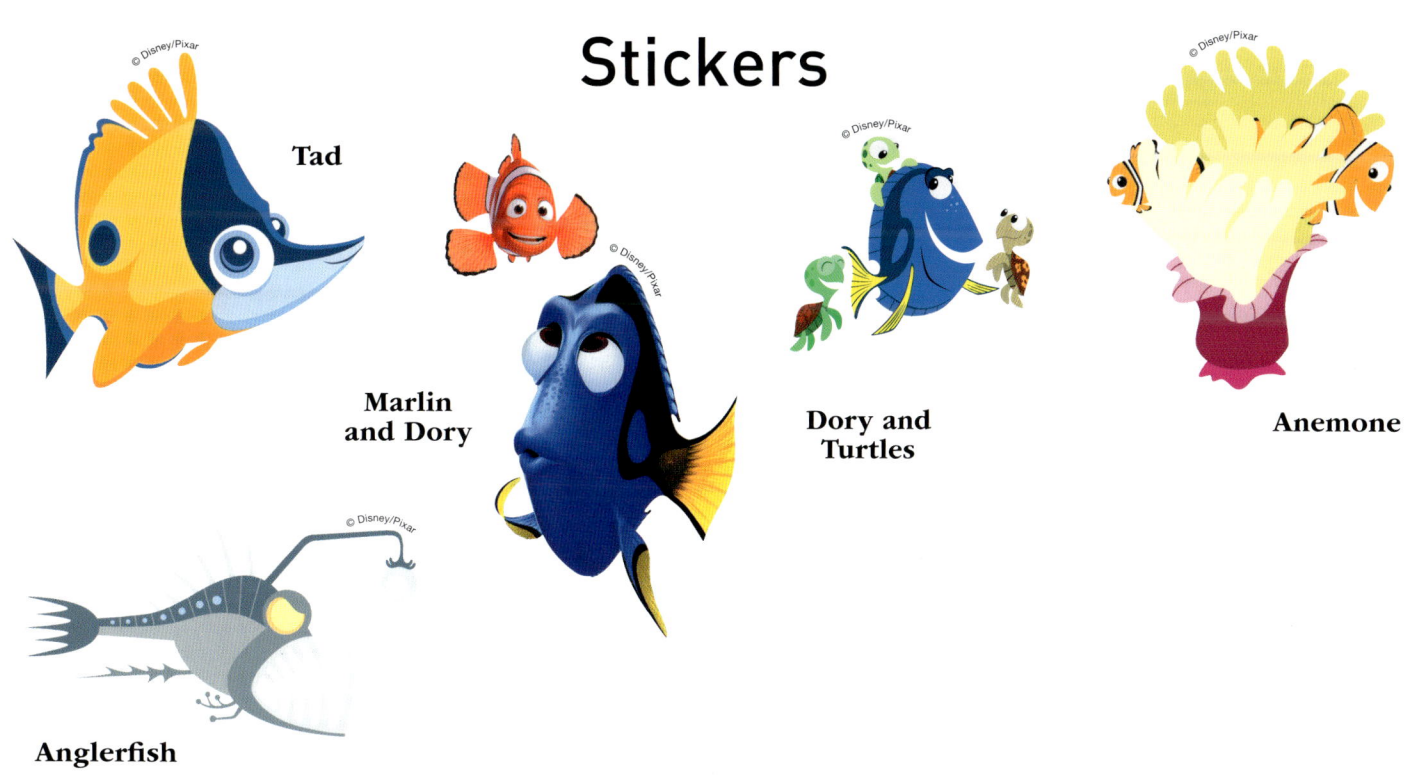

Tad · Marlin and Dory · Dory and Turtles · Anemone

Anglerfish

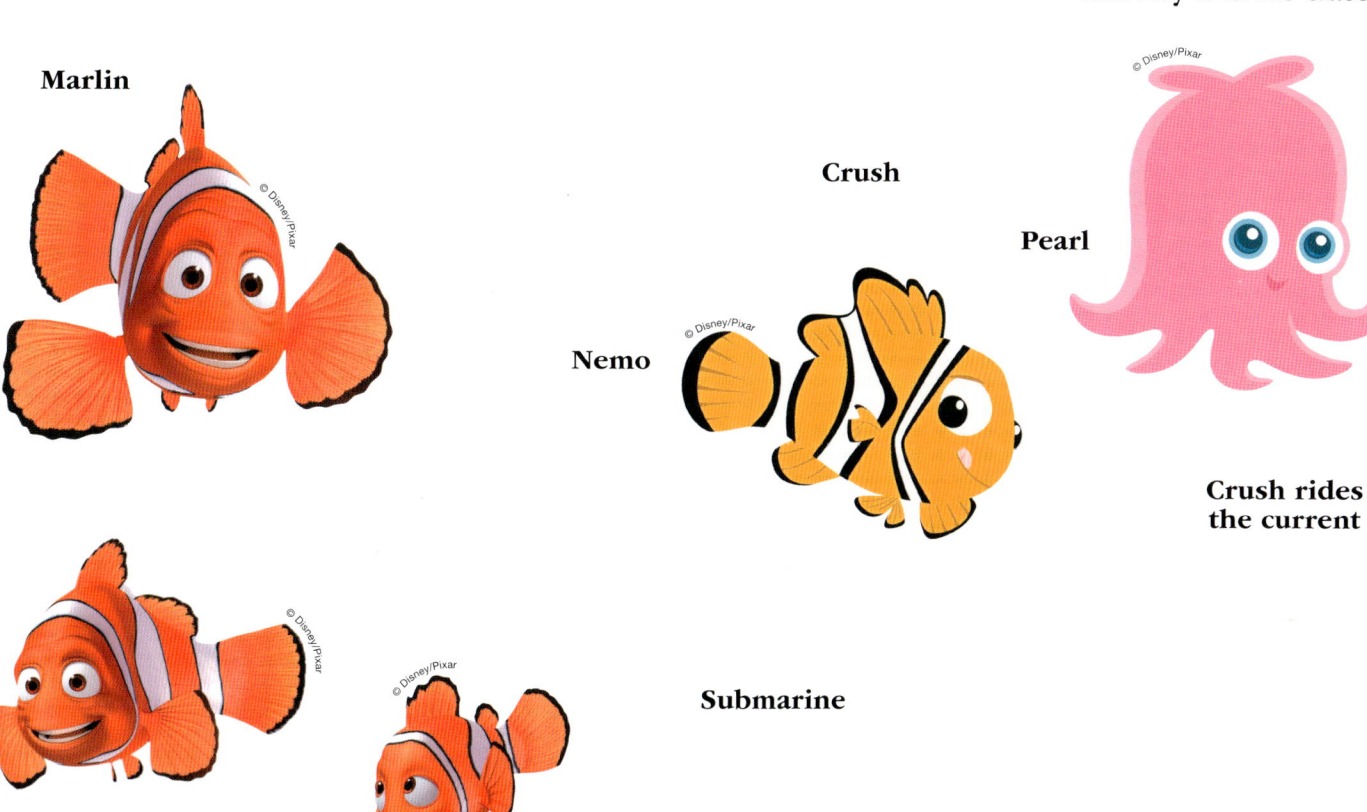

Marlin · Mr. Ray and his class · Crush · Pearl · Nemo · Crush rides the current · Marlin · Submarine

A Jellyfish forest

Bruce